SPOTLIGHT ON SPACE SCIENCE

JOURNEY TO NEPTUNE

SØ-ANG-356

D1447812

NOAH BROCKMAN

PowerKiDS press™

New York

VERNON AREA PUBLIC LIBRARY
LINCOLNSHIRE, IL 60069
www.vapld.info

Published in 2015 by The Rosen Publishing Group, Inc.
29 East 21st Street, New York, NY 10010

Copyright © 2015 by The Rosen Publishing Group, Inc.

All rights reserved. No part of this book may be reproduced in any form without permission in writing from the publisher, except by a reviewer.

First Edition

Editor: Susan Meyer
Book Design: Kris Everson

Photo Credits: Cover (all), pp. 8, 9, 14, 15, 16, 17, 19 (both), 20, 22, 24, 26 NASA; pp. 5, 27 NASA/JPL; pp. 6, 29 Shutterstock.com; p. 7 NASA, Donald Walter (South Carolina State University), Paul Scowen and Brian Moore (Arizona State University); p. 10 European Southern Observatory; p. 11 DETLEV VAN RAVENSWAAY/Science Photo Library/Getty Images; p. 13 Yutthaphong/ Shutterstock.com; pp. 21, 23 NASA/JPL/USGS; p. 25 © iStockphoto.com/larslentz.

Library of Congress Cataloging-in-Publication Data

Brockman, Noah.
Journey to Neptune / by Noah Brockman.
p. cm. — (Spotlight on space science)
Includes index.
ISBN 978-1-4994-0374-9 (pbk.)
ISBN 978-1-4994-0403-6 (6-pack)
ISBN 978-1-4994-0424-1 (library binding)
1. Neptune (Planet) — Juvenile literature. I. Title.
QB691.B78 2015
523.48—d23

Manufactured in the United States of America

CPSIA Compliance Information: Batch #CW15PK: For Further Information contact Rosen Publishing, New York, New York at 1-800-237-9932

CONTENTS

A DISTANT, STORMY PLANET
CHAPTER 1

Neptune is the most distant planet from the Sun in our **solar system**. It **orbits** the Sun at an average distance of 2.8 billion miles (4.5 billion km). That's about 30 times further from the Sun than Earth.

The five planets nearest to Earth—Mercury, Venus, Mars, Jupiter, and Saturn—can be seen with the naked eye. Ancient **astronomers** watched and studied these planets for thousands of years. Neptune is too far from Earth to be seen without a telescope, however. Astronomers did not know this planet existed until the mid-1800s.

Today, we know Neptune is home to massive storms. We know it has many moons and is made mostly of gases and liquids. Only one spacecraft has ever visited the planet, though, so we still have much to learn about this icy, distant world.

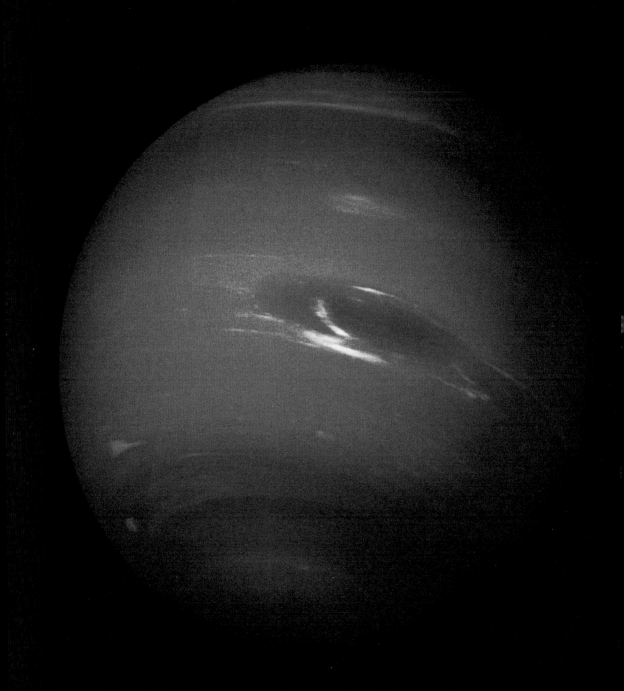

People did not get a close look at Neptune's stormy blue surface until 143 years after its discovery.

5

HOW NEPTUNE FORMED

CHAPTER 2

The planets in our solar system were created when our Sun formed about 4.5 billion years ago.

This illustration shows the moment when our Sun ignited to become a **star**.

Before our solar system formed, there was a huge cloud of gas and dust floating in space. Over time, part of the cloud collapsed on itself, forming a massive spinning sphere, or ball. Around the sphere, a disk formed from the remaining gas and dust. The sphere pulled in more gas and dust, adding to its size, weight, and **gravity**. Pressure built up as the material in the sphere was pressed together by gravity, causing the sphere's core to heat up and reach temperatures of around 18,000,000°F (10,000,000°C). Finally, the temperature inside the sphere became so

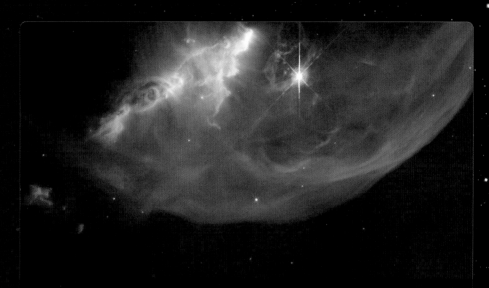

This is part of the Bubble Nebula. A nebula is a cloud of gas and dust where stars are born.

hot that it ignited. A new star, our Sun, was born!

Gas and dust continued to spin in a disk around the Sun. Over time, the leftover matter from the formation of the Sun clumped together to form the solar system's planets, their moons, **asteroids**, and every other object in our solar system.

Mercury is the closest planet to the Sun. Next comes Venus, then Earth, Mars, Jupiter, Saturn, Uranus, and finally Neptune.

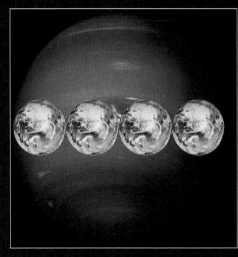

This diagram compares the size of Neptune to Earth.

It can be difficult to imagine the sizes of the planets. One fun way to compare them is to think of the Sun as a bowling ball. Using that scale, Mercury and Mars would be the size of pinheads compared to the bowling ball–sized Sun. Venus and Earth would be the size of peppercorns. Uranus and Neptune would be the size of peas, while Saturn would be the size of a marble. Jupiter, the largest of the planets, would be the size of a chestnut.

The solar system's eight planets do not all have the same structure. Mercury, Venus, Earth, and Mars formed with solid, rocky surfaces. Jupiter, Saturn, Uranus, and Neptune, the furthest planets from the Sun, are made mostly of gas and do not have solid surfaces. They're known as the gas giants.

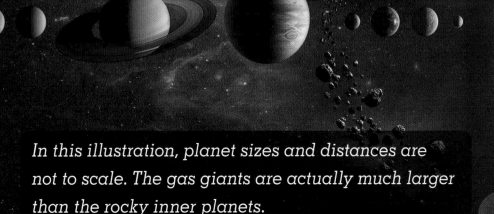

In this illustration, planet sizes and distances are not to scale. The gas giants are actually much larger than the rocky inner planets.

ACROSS GREAT DISTANCES

CHAPTER 4

Each of the planets in our solar system is orbiting the Sun. The solar system is so vast, however, that it can be hard to imagine the distances between the

This artwork shows how the Sun might look from Neptune and the surface of Triton, which is Neptune's largest moon.

planets when those distances are measured in millions or billions of miles (km).

So how can we imagine the enormous distances between the Sun and the planets, especially the outer planets such as Neptune? If we once again think of the Sun as a bowling ball, our peppercorn-sized Earth would be about 26 yards (24 m) from the Sun. Faraway pea-sized Neptune, however, would be 777 yards (710 m) from the Sun. That's more than seven football fields away!

In 1977, two NASA spacecraft, *Voyager 1* and *Voyager 2*, left Earth. By spring 2011, the *Voyagers* had made it to the outer regions of our solar system. Even though they're traveling at speeds of about 34,000 miles per hour (54,700 km/h), the two spacecraft still took over 30 years just to reach the edge of our solar system.

This illustration shows the orbits of the planets around the Sun. Their distances are not to scale.

THE EARLIEST OBSERVATIONS
CHAPTER 5

For centuries, astronomers knew of five planets that could be seen from Earth with the naked eye. Then, in 1781, Uranus became the first planet to be discovered by an astronomer using a telescope.

Urbain Joseph Le Verrier

German-born British astronomer William Herschel discovered Uranus while looking for stars in March 1781. When he first observed the planet, he believed it was a star or perhaps a **comet**.

Just over 50 years later, Neptune was discovered using a combination of math calculations and a telescope. A French mathematician named Urbain Joseph Le Verrier predicted the existence of Neptune when he noticed that the gravity of a

A statue of the Roman god Neptune

large object was affecting the orbit of Uranus. Le Verrier sent his calculations to a German astronomer, Johann Gottfried Galle. Using Le Verrier's information, Galle searched for the mysterious object using a telescope. He found Neptune on his first night of searching in September 1846.

A VERY LONG YEAR!

CHAPTER 6

Like Earth and every other object in the solar system, distant Neptune orbits the Sun. As it travels through space, it moves at about 12,000 miles per hour (19,300 km/h).

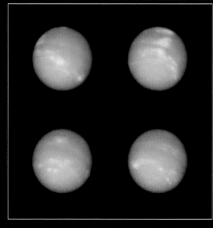

In 2011, Neptune completed its first full orbit around the Sun since its discovery. The Hubble Space Telescope captured these images to commemorate the event.

The time period that it takes a planet to make one full orbit of the Sun is called a year. Earth orbits the Sun once every 365 days, so a year on Earth is 365 days. Neptune's journey takes much longer, however, because it is so much farther from the Sun. In order to make one full orbit around the Sun, Neptune must travel 17.5 billion miles (28.2 billion km). This incredible journey

The Hubble Space Telescope orbits Earth outside of our atmosphere.

takes 60,190 days. So, a year on Neptune is nearly 165 Earth years long!

As each planet orbits the Sun, it also spins, or rotates, on its **axis**. Earth rotates once every 24 hours. Neptune rotates faster than Earth, though, and makes one full rotation every 16 hours.

BENEATH NEPTUNE'S ATMOSPHERE

CHAPTER 7

As one of the gas giants, Neptune does not have a solid surface like Earth or Mars. This planet is made mostly of gases and liquids.

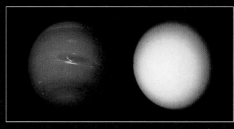

These images of Neptune (left) and Uranus (right) were taken by *Voyager 2*. Both planets look blue because of the methane in their atmospheres, but what causes their colors to be so different?

Under a layer of clouds, Neptune has an atmosphere of hydrogen, helium, and methane gases. The methane in the planet's atmosphere (and how it behaves with the Sun's light) is what gives Neptune its blue color. Light is made up of different colors. When the Sun's light hits Neptune's atmosphere, the methane absorbs the red parts of the light, but reflects the blues and greens, so we see Neptune as blue. Uranus gets its blue color in exactly the same way. Neptune is a much brighter blue than Uranus, however,

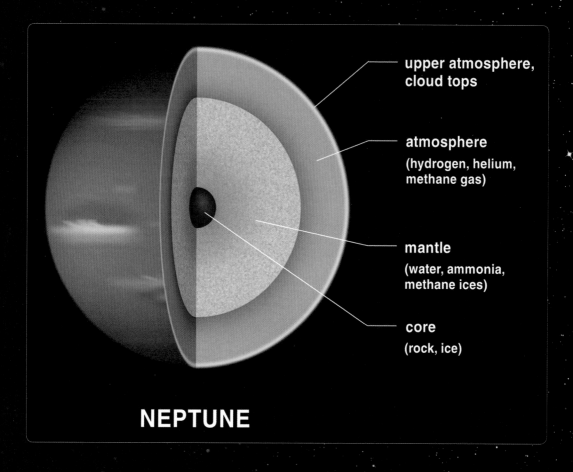

upper atmosphere, cloud tops

atmosphere
(hydrogen, helium, methane gas)

mantle
(water, ammonia, methane ices)

core
(rock, ice)

NEPTUNE

so scientists still need to discover what causes the difference in the planets' colors.

Beneath Neptune's atmosphere are layers of icy liquid hydrogen, helium, methane, water, and ammonia. Scientists believe there is a solid core of rock and ice about the size of Earth at the center of the planet.

EXTREME WEATHER

The Sun is the driving force behind the many different types of weather we experience on Earth. You would therefore expect that Neptune, which is so much further from the Sun, would simply be icy cold with very little weather. That is not the case, however.

Storms hurtle around Neptune, and winds have been recorded at speeds of up to 1,500 miles per hour (2,400 km/h). That's over 10 times the windspeed of the very worst hurricanes here on Earth!

When *Voyager 2* visited Neptune in 1989, it witnessed a huge storm in progress that scientists named the Great Dark Spot. The hurricane-like storm was large enough to contain our Earth. When the Hubble Space Telescope viewed Neptune in 1994, the storm was gone. This was interesting to astronomers

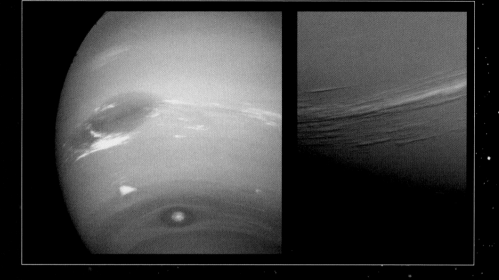

Voyager 2 snapped this photograph (left) of the Great Dark Spot, which was moving at about 750 miles per hour (1,200 km/h), and a smaller storm below called Dark Spot 2. The second photograph shows streaks of clouds high in Neptune's atmosphere.

because a giant storm named the Great Red Spot has been raging on Jupiter for over 400 years. Neptune's storms seem to form and die down much faster, showing how changeable the planet's weather

NEPTUNE'S MANY MOONS

CHAPTER 9

Just 17 days after Johann
Gottfried Galle discovered
Neptune in September 1846,
the planet's largest moon,
Triton, was discovered by a
British astronomer named
William Lassell.

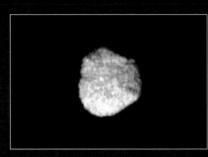

Neptune's moon Proteus has a
lumpy, irregular shape.

In 1949, over 100 years later, American astronomer
Gerard Kuiper discovered Neptune's third-largest
moon, Nereid. Nereid has a diameter of just 210
miles (340 km) and is so far from Neptune that it
takes 360 days to make one orbit of the planet.

When *Voyager 2* visited Neptune 40 years
later, it discovered the planet's second-largest
moon, Proteus, and five other smaller moons.
Even though Proteus, with a diameter of 260
miles (420 km), is larger than Nereid, it was too
difficult to see from Earth because it is one of the

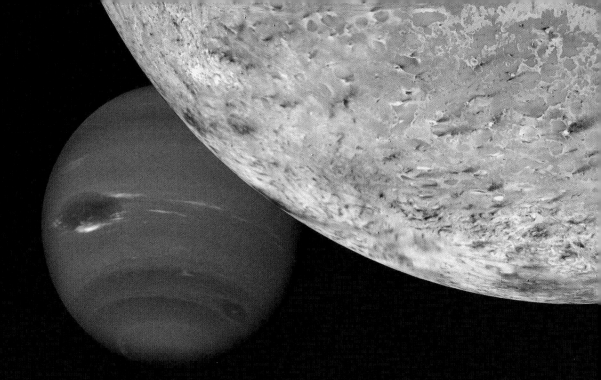

Triton with a view of Neptune

darkest objects in the solar system. The little moon is covered in craters caused by collisions with other space objects.

As technology has improved, astronomers using telescopes on Earth have been able to find more moons orbiting Neptune. At the beginning of 2013, Neptune had a total of 13 known moons.

THE LARGEST MOON

CHAPTER 10

Neptune's largest moon, Triton, is about three-quarters the size of Earth's moon. It has a diameter of 1,680 miles (2,700 km). Triton orbits Neptune in the opposite direction to which the planet is rotating. This is

This scene showing the surface of Triton was created by computers using data from *Voyager 2*.

unusual for a large moon and makes scientists think the moon did not form alongside the planet. It is possible that Triton is an object from a region in space named the **Kuiper Belt** and was captured by Neptune's gravity and pulled into orbit around the planet.

Triton's crust is made of frozen nitrogen. Beneath the crust is a layer of liquids and ice surrounding a core of rock and metal. Icy liquids, believed to

This composite image from the Voyager mission shows what Neptune would look like if you were standing on Triton.

be nitrogen and methane, burst from the moon's crust through cryovolcanoes, or ice volcanoes. This material can travel miles (km) into the cold atmosphere surrounding the moon. Then the liquids freeze and snow back down onto the moon's surface.

ROCKY RINGS

About a week before William Lassell discovered Triton in 1846, he believed he saw a ring around Neptune. What Lassell in fact saw was a distortion of light caused by his telescope.

This image shows Saturn's rings with colors added by a computer. Saturn's thick, multiple rings can easily be observed from Earth with a telescope, while Neptune's thin, faint rings are very difficult to see.

When *Voyager 2* visited Neptune nearly 150 years later, however, it discovered that, like the other gas giants, Neptune does indeed have rings. To date, six rings have been discovered encircling Neptune.

Neptune's rings are made of dust and pieces of rock. Unlike Saturn's vast, showy rings, Neptune's rings are thin, dark, and very difficult to see. In

This illustration shows how the rings of Neptune might look up close.

places, the material in the rings clumps together to form thicker areas called arcs.

Very little is known about Neptune's rings, but scientists believe they may only be a few million years old. They may also not be a permanent feature, but might be forming and then breaking apart, unlike Saturn's more permanent system of rings.

VOYAGER 2

CHAPTER 12

Only one spacecraft, *Voyager 2*, has ever visited Neptune. *Voyager 2* and its sister ship, *Voyager 1*, began their mission to visit the solar system's gas giants in 1977.

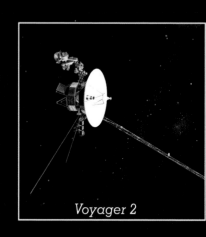

Voyager 2

The mission was possible because the orbits of Jupiter, Saturn, Uranus, and Neptune were **aligned** in a way that only happens every 175 years. This rare alignment allowed the spacecraft to visit a planet and then use the gravity of that planet like a slingshot to propel them on to their next destination.

Voyager 2 launched from the Kennedy Space Center at Cape Canaveral, Florida, on August 20, 1977. *Voyager 1* actually launched after *Voyager 2* on September 5, 1977.

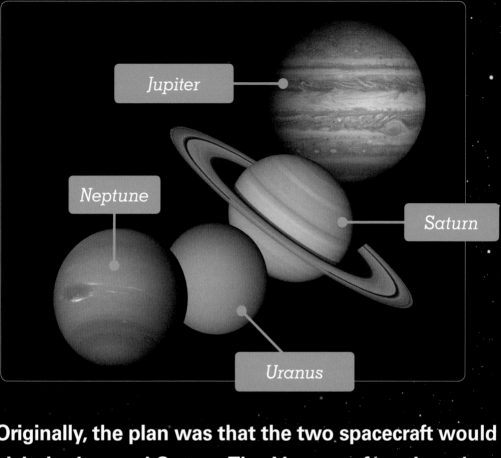

Jupiter

Neptune

Saturn

Uranus

Originally, the plan was that the two spacecraft would visit Jupiter and Saturn. The *Voyagers* functioned so successfully, however, that it became possible to extend their missions. *Voyager 2* visited Jupiter, then Saturn, and when it was found that its instruments were still functioning well, its mission was extended to include Uranus. After a five-and-a-half-hour flyby of Uranus, *Voyager 2* was set on a course for Neptune.

CONTINUING EXPLORATION
CHAPTER 13

Voyager 2 had traveled over 4.3 billion miles (7 billion km) when it reached distant Neptune on August 25, 1989. At its closest, *Voyager 2* flew just 3,075 miles (4,950 km) above Neptune's cloud tops. During its visit, it discovered previously unknown moons and the planet's rings. The spacecraft measured wind speeds on Neptune and collected data that showed the chemical makeup of the planet. Finally, *Voyager 2* flew by Triton, revealing that the moon is home to cryovolcanoes and is one of the coldest places in the solar system.

After saying goodbye to Triton, *Voyager 2* was set on course for the outer reaches of the solar system and beyond, deeper into our galaxy, the Milky Way. Its mission continues to this day!

In the future, new spacecraft will reveal the secrets of Neptune, its rings, and its many moons.

While *Voyager 2*'s flyby of Neptune only lasted a matter of hours, without it, very little would be known about Neptune. Books such as this would have far less information to give, and few pictures of the faraway, blue world!

GLOSSARY

aligned: Positioned in a straight line.

asteroid: A small, rocky body that orbits the Sun.

astronomer: A person who studies space objects.

atmosphere: The blanket of gases that surrounds the surface of a planet or moon.

axis: An imaginary straight line around which a planet turns.

comet: A space object made of ice and dust with a tail that points away from the Sun.

gravity: The force that pulls an object toward the center of another object that has mass.

Kuiper Belt: A region of the solar system beyond Neptune where comets and other icy bodies orbit the Sun.

orbit: To move around an object along a curved path; also, the curved path of a space object around a star or planet.

solar system: The Sun and the space bodies that move around it, including the planets and their moons.

star: A space object made of gases that produces its own light.

FOR MORE INFORMATION

BOOKS

Aguilar, David A. *Space Encyclopedia: A Tour of Our Solar System and Beyond.* Washington, D.C.: National Geographic, 2013.

Jackson, Tom. *Our Solar System: A Nonfiction Companion to the Original Magic School Bus Series.* New York, NY: Scholastic, 2014.

Roza, Greg. *Neptune: The Stormy Planet.* New York, NY: Gareth Stevens Publishing, 2010.

WEBSITES

Due to the changing nature of Internet links, PowerKids Press has developed an online list of websites related to the subject of this book. This site is updated regularly. Please use this link to access the list: www.powerkidslinks.com/soss/nept

INDEX

VERNON AREA PUBLIC LIBRARY
LINCOLNSHIRE, IL 60069
www.vapld.info